Among the Lilies

Among the Lilies

A White Lotus Anthology

Edited by

Marie Summers
an'ya
Harriot West
Francis Masat
Bette Wappner (b'oki)

Among the Lilies
A White Lotus Anthology

White Lotus

Shadow Poetry © 2008
ISBN 978-0-6152-1045-2

Shadow Poetry
1209 Milwaukee Street
Excelsior Springs, MO 64024 USA
www.shadowpoetry.com

Front Cover Sumi-e: Origa
Back Cover Haiga: Isira Sananda & Allison Millcock
Block Carvings: Bette Wappner (b'oki)
Interior Haiga: Origa, Geert Verbeke, Jan Turner, and
       Laryalee Fraser
Interior Artwork: Jan Turner, John Hawkhead, Margaret
       R. Smith, and Sandy Ellis
Interior Photographs: Mike Rehling, Jenny Ovaere,
       James Patrick Haynes, and Margaret R. Smith

Printed in the United States of America
Published – May 2008

move aside
cloud and fog!
lotuses are blooming

Issa, 1814

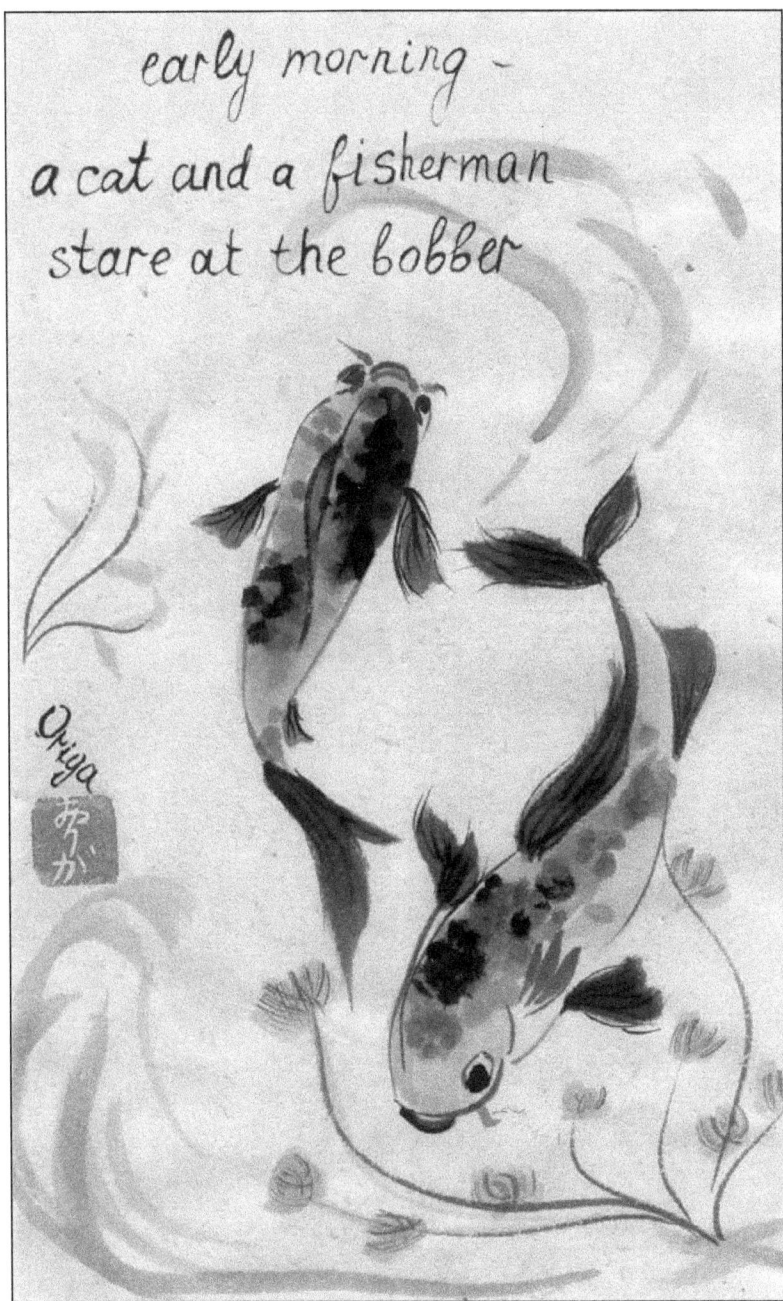

early morning –
a cat and a fisherman
stare at the bobber

Contents

Haiku/Senryu

first lotus bloom
a Buddhist monk raises
his hands to the sky

Theresa Thompson

breast high
in a private pond
white lilies

an'ya

lily pond —
not big enough
for the moon

Željko Funda

holding the first rays
of morning light
water lily

Tony A. Thompson

loneliness . . .
the white lotus nestles
a dew drop

Magdalena Dale

in the ripples
bobbing—
some lily

Ed Baker

Artwork by Jan Turner

ancient evening
he carves in stone
a white lotus

William Scott Galasso

old woman
and lotus leaves
bow low to the pond

Margaret Chula

gentle wind
water lilies catch
a drifting boat

Glenn G. Coats

lotus lilies
around the upturned tail
of a B-52
      Hanoi, Vietnam, 2000

Steve Dolphy

a lily bud
swells underwater—
unspoken thoughts

Peggy Willis Lyles

summer night—
blossoming in the pond,
water lilies and stars

Anatoly Kudryavitsky

(c) Illustration & haiku Geert Verbeke

the lotus
grows out of the mud -
wordless

brief shower—
quicksilver
on a lotus cup

H. F. Noyes

white water lilies—
a buffalo takes a bath
under their glimmer

Vasile Moldovan

water lilies . . .
the space between
two bridge planks

Kala Ramesh

Photograph by Jenny Ovaere

lily of the nile
one of the children
colours it blue

Radhey Shiam

marked with henna
her hands present
the white lotus

William Scott Galasso

sunrise—
the popping sound
of a water lily

Emily Romano

Artwork by Margaret R. Smith

raindrops—
circles meet
beyond the lily pads

Elaine Riddell

water lilies
a few red underleaves
tipped up

Bruce Ross

lily-white flower
playing
just so

Ed Baker

In fading light,
I join the lilies
for vespers.

alexis rotella

a white lotus—
all around it
light from light

Vasile Moldovan

moving closer—
the designs on her kurta
turn into lilies

Kala Ramesh

toy warship
pushed out
   among lily pads

   Patricia Neubauer

evening star—
a lotus turns
above a shadow

   Francis Masat

morning mist—
the yellow of a lily
showing through the bud

   Peggy Willis Lyles

a lotus flower
transcends
its muddy pond

Elaine Riddell

white lily . . .
swan song ripples
the pond

Magdalena Dale

floating purple—
my daydreams follow
the water hyacinth

Deborah P Kolodji

Photograph by Mike Rehling

water hyacinth
my friends mourn
their daughter

Deborah P Kolodji

diving merganser
in the summer night:
a lotus in bloom

Vasile Moldovan

Artwork by Jan Turner

cropped lily stems
at the pond's edge—
tracks from a moose

H. F. Noyes

fragile water-lilies
being taken care of by
the palm of the lake

Bozena Zernec

finding my own path . . .
a muskrat parts
the lily pads

Margaret R. Smith

lotus rising—
mystic vortex
sings my name

Jan Turner

Artwork by Jan Turner

lotus blossoms
faces pressed
to a bus window

Bob Lucky

night pond—
a first star's
silent ping

H. F. Noyes

small pool
a gull appears . . .
disappears

Winona Baker

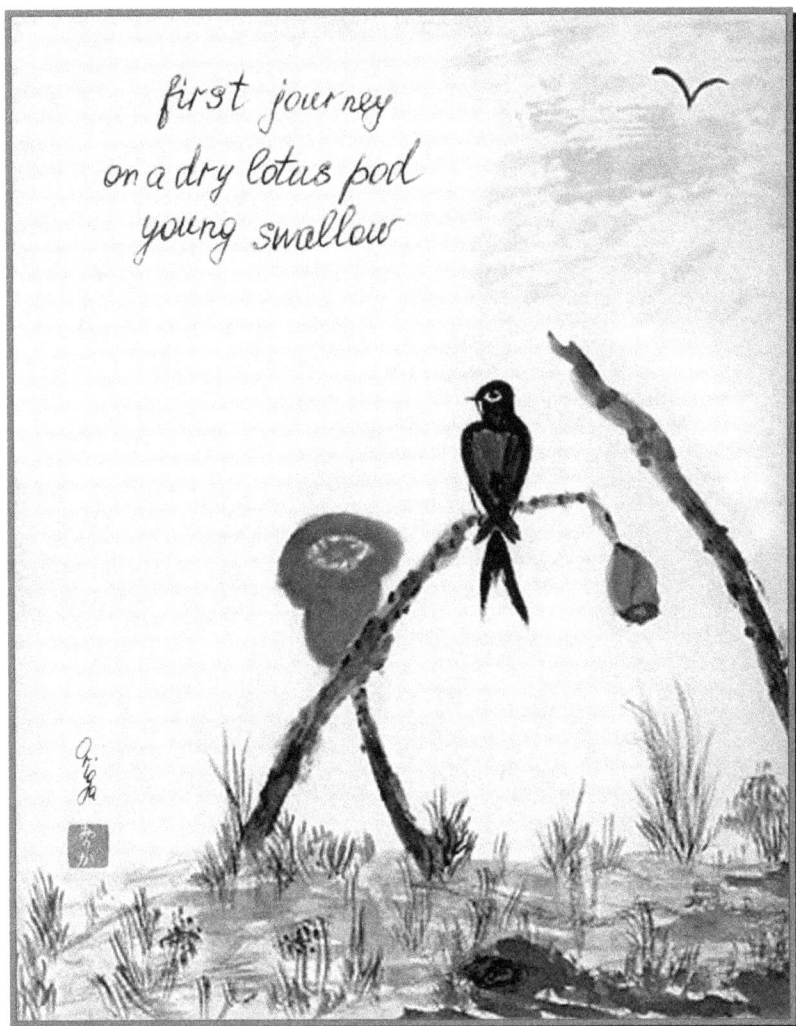

first journey
on a dry lotus pod
young swallow

cool light
fills the lily pond—
winter moon

Sylvia Forges-Ryan

by her bedside
a sprig of bamboo
in pond water

Janelle Barrera

before the storm
in the bottom of the lake
peaks of clouds

Vasile Moldovan

the same train
the same lotus pond
charm me everyday

Radhey Shiam

lily pond
an earthworm
disturbs the moon

Ernest J. Berry

decayed leaves
the pond
their color

Margaret Chula

summer silence
the hum of insects
over the pond

André Surridge

lily-choked pond
the fisherman casts his line
beyond the moon

Bob Lucky

country pond
a hedgehog drinks
from the moon

Željko Funda

he plays the bass –
his subdued tribute
to the lily pond

(c) Haiga: Geert Verbeke

lily pond—
a Modigliani squiggle
seams the surface

H. F. Noyes

skittering breezes—
colors of the dragon kite
cross the carp pond

H. F. Noyes

willows greening
a killdeer curves
over the glassy pond

Elizabeth Howard

lily pond . . .
among the stars
stepping stones

Elinor Pihl Huggett

twilight
the pond holds it
the longest

Jim Kacian

in thick water
a wild sow
chewing

Dubravko Korbus

summer evening
in the pool
a lily pinkens

Katrina Shepherd

in the depth
of the lily pond
the halo moon

Vasile Moldovan

last night's dream
near the pond's edge
the glow of a firefly

Sylvia Forges-Ryan

a light at her window—
last night's star is back
in the lily pond

H. F. Noyes

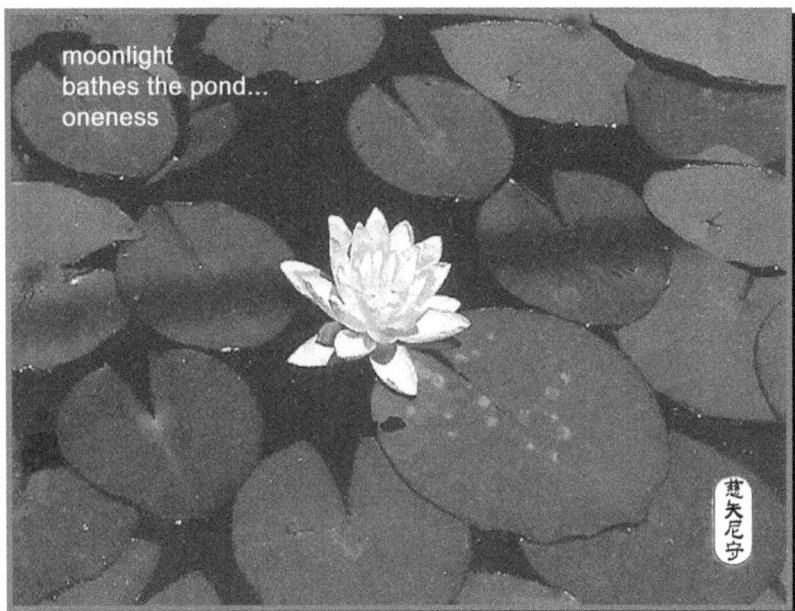

moonlight
bathes the pond...
oneness

Haiga by Jan Turner

just one star
on the lily pond . . .
a thistle seed

Diana Webb

between winter storms
steam rises
off the lily pond

Renée Owen

at the pond's centre
a circle of ripples
    around the full moon

John Hawkhead

autumn wind
covers the pond
leaf by leaf

Sylvia Forges-Ryan

Photograph by James Patrick Haynes

a single raindrop
in the lily pond
many ripples

Katrina Shepherd

Artwork by Margaret R. Smith

news of your illness . . .
gray clouds hold steady
over the pond

Marie Summers

placid pond
in the moon's reflection
kabuki dance

Connie Marcum Wong

moonlight
tiny waves sway thick walls
of the castle

Bozena Zernec

trisected
by tall reeds,
blue heron

William Scott Galasso

a heron's eye—
the branch with a lizard
now bare

Francis Masat

far from the pond
two blue herons
in the winter brown field

Patricia Neubauer

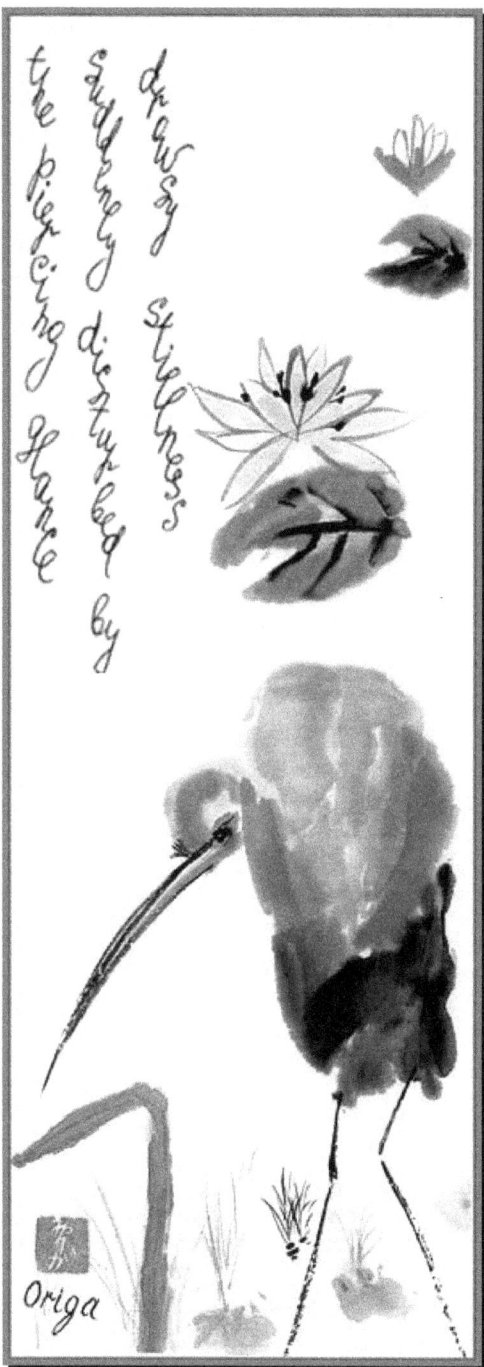

drowsy
stillness
suddenly
disturbed
by
the piercing glance

Origa

in the stillness
of water plants
a mallard's blue flash

H. F. Noyes

summer is leaving —
a white heron hurries
along the pond

Origa

winter dusk —
a grey heron disappears
in the mist

D. V. Rozic

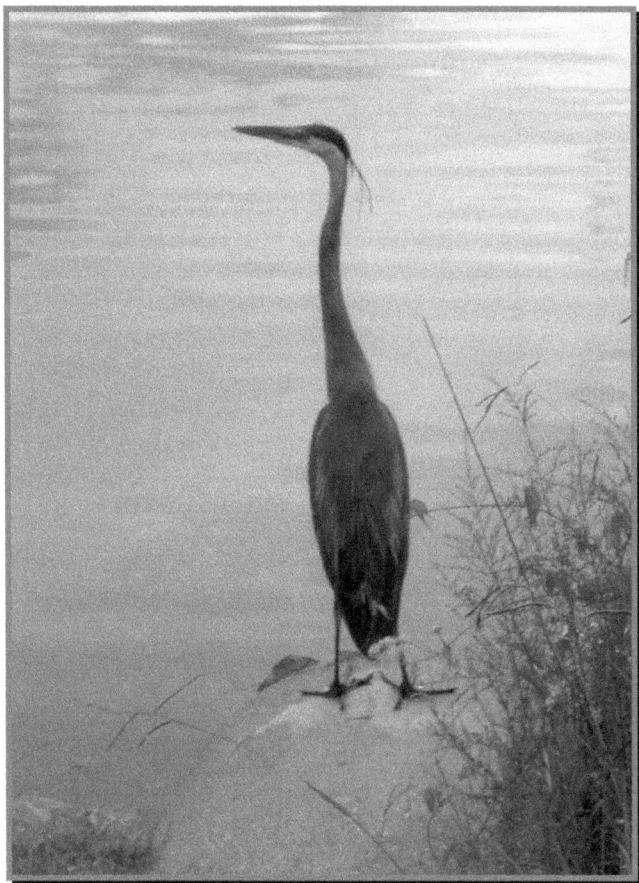

Photograph by Margaret R. Smith

summer grass
a stork's neck waves
its red beak

Stjepan Rozic

by a lily pad
one duckling
then two

Susan Sanchez-Barnett

thick fog
rising off the pond . . .
flock of geese

Marie Summers

sultry afternoon—
the lizard's tail sways
with the heron's flight

Linda Jeannette Ward

night
deepening
the frog pond

Carolyn Thomas

far beyond
frog
moon also

Ed Baker

noon pond
the eyes of frogs
here and there

Zeljhka Vucinic-Jambresic

far beyond
flower
frog leaps

Ed Baker

days of rain—
only the frogs
seem glad

Taft Chatham

first sign of spring
my mother hears frogs
for my father

Glenn G. Coats

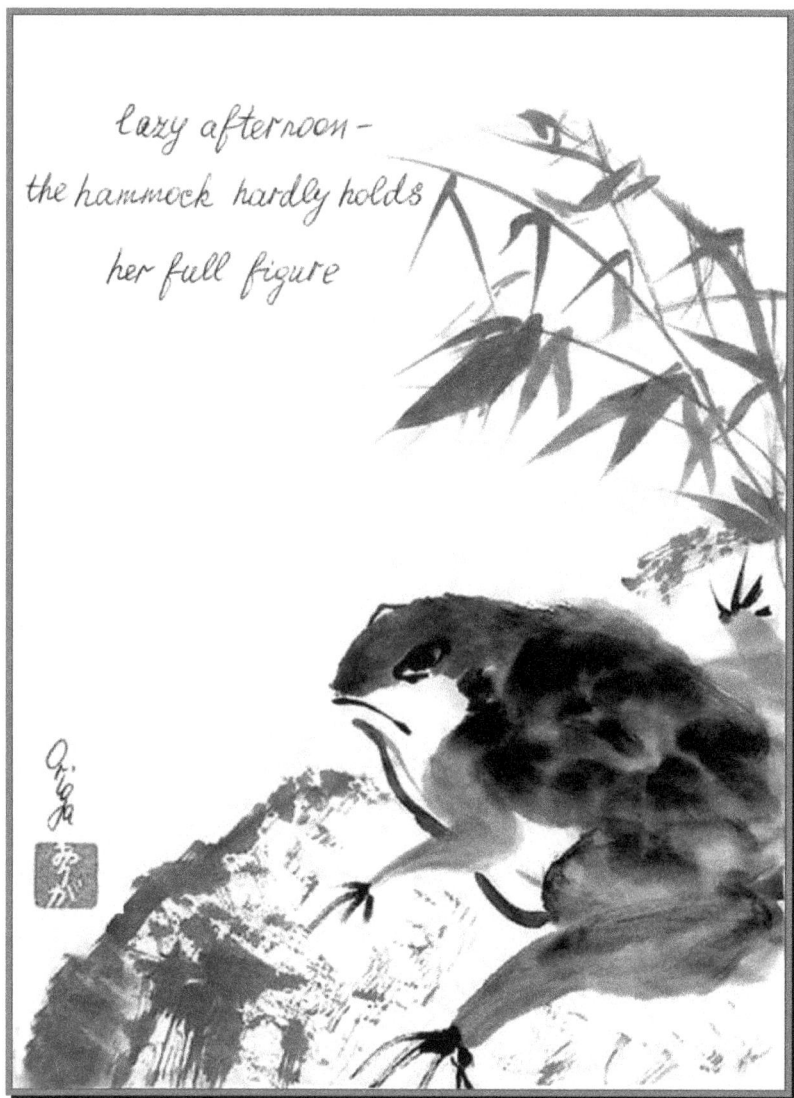

lazy afternoon—
the hammock hardly holds
her full figure

a frog
lifts the pond
on its legs

Zeljhka Vucinic-Jambresic

croak of a bullfrog
my real home
far away

Fonda Bell Miller

making no sound . . .
light rain sweeps in
on the chorus of frogs

H. F. Noyes

first day of summer
a frog's croak
lengthens

Glenn G. Coats

summer rain . . .
the frog pees
in my hand

Stanford M. Forrester

moonset
in the pond
only frogs and stars

Vasile Moldovan

crack of a bough
the frog jumps into
the sinking moon

Stjepan Rozic

Artwork by John Hawkhead

early dusk –
frog's chorus pierces
the air

the whole pond
in the frog's eyes
blink!

Jim Kacian

morning blossom
on the water lily
spotted frog

Bozena Zernec

humid evening
a frog's croak ripples
across the pond

Susan Sanchez-Barnett

bullfrog
year-after-year
on her pad

Ed Baker

lily pad
the tiny turtle gains
a foothold

Emily Romano

Japanese garden
the perched turtle
part of the stone

Bruce Ross

Artwork by Jan Turner

hatching turtle—
I, too, come out
of my shell

Margaret R. Smith

a dragonfly
was on the lily pad
before that swallow

Winona Baker

sunrise
the dragonfly
drags its shadow off

Bob Lucky

midsummer heat
a dragonfly dips her mate
into the pond

Jim Kacian

touching
a dragonfly's wing
thunder

Tony A. Thompson

orange dragonfly
over the koi pond
Hiroshima Day

Deborah P Kolodji

how far do they wander
from the lily pond?
dragonflies

Janelle Barrera

lily pad
the holding pattern
of dragonflies

Ernest J. Berry

dragonfly . . .
a picnic
long ago

Shawn Bowman

reflecting
on the pond's reflections
dragonfly and I

Margaret Chula

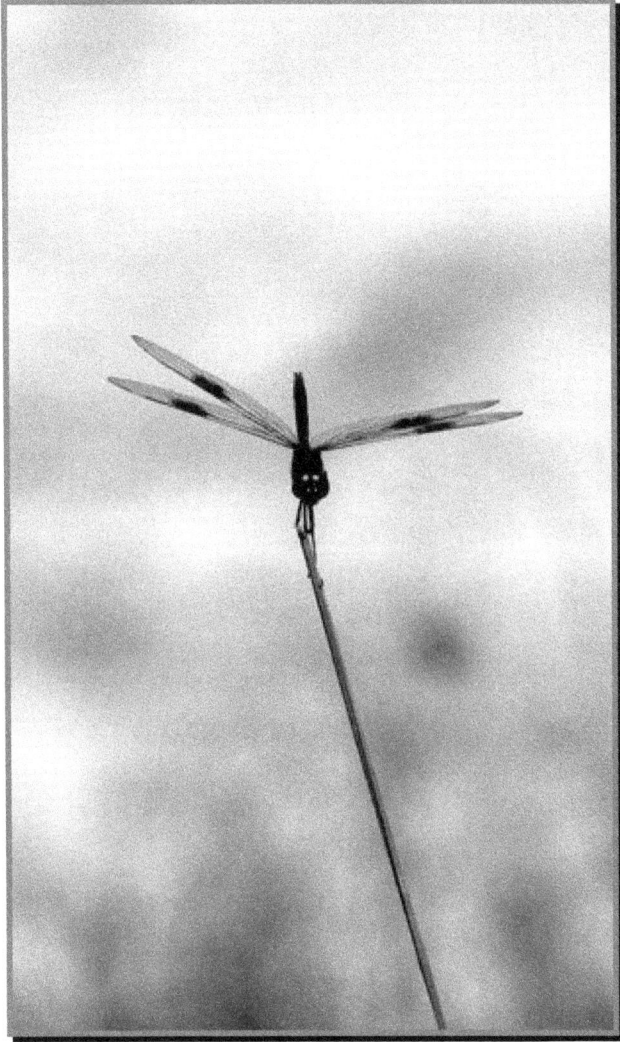

Photograph by Mike Rehling

daydreaming . . .
a damselfly lands
on my finger

Susan Constable

dragonfly
on a water lily
studying stillness

Margarita Engle

lighter than water
the dragonfly lands
on the moon

Marie Summers

for a moment
on the wildflower's sway . . .
blue dragonfly

Stanford M. Forrester

slow bend in the stream—
in the heron's still eye
blue-green dragonflies

John Hawkhead

high noon
dragonfly shadows crosshatch
the lily pond

Elizabeth Howard

dragonfly . . .
the tai chi master
shifts his stance

Peggy Willis Lyles

circling lower
between the clouds
a dragonfly

Susan Sanchez-Barnett

soft breeze
the dragonfly carcass
rocks wing to wing

Bob Lucky

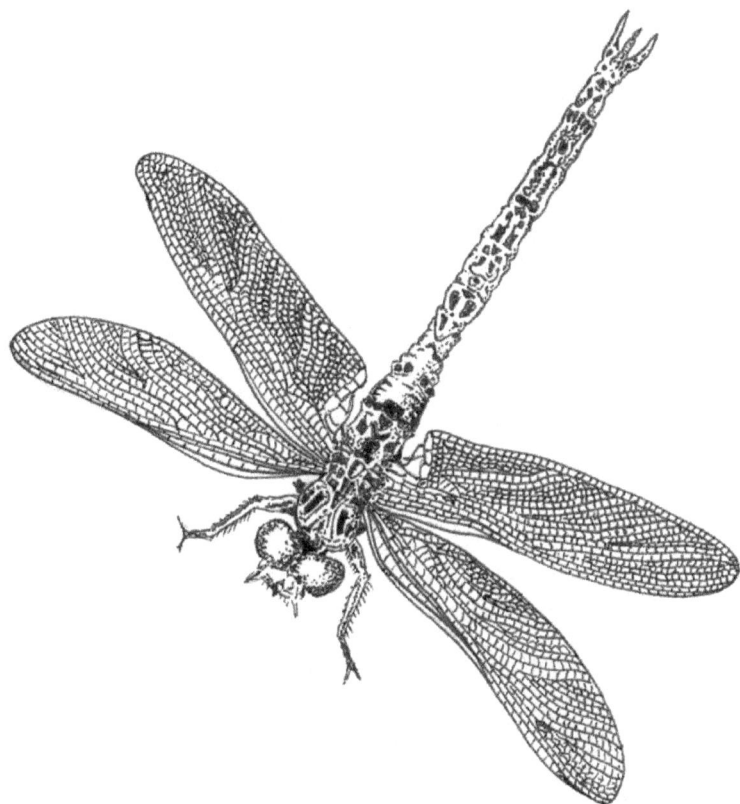

Artwork by John Hawkhead

last night's rain . . .
the dragonfly
one twig higher

Dubravko Korbus

a dragonfly . . .
the rattle of mill wheels
in both eyes

Boris Nazansky

two blue dragonflies
hover over the pond . . .
their calm reflections

Carolyn Thomas

formal lotus pond
a blue dragonfly perched
on an empty stem

Bruce Ross

vernal dawn –
light breeze takes away
   my dream

   . . .

светает –
ветерок уносит
   мою мечту

foggy mountain pond
each dragonfly pauses
at the clearing

Bruce Ross

blue damselfly
over the water lilies
daydreams

Deborah P Kolodji

marshland
a dragonfly hovers above
its shadow

Zeljhka Vucinic-Jambresic

dragonfly
over the still pond
his shadow remains

(for David Priebe)

Tony A. Thompson

shiny penny . . .
a dragonfly hovers
over my wish

Marie Summers

dipping three times
into the lily pond
blue dragonfly

Sharon Hammer Baker

pond edge—
darting sideways
a blue damselfly

André Surridge

afternoon breeze
the passing shade
of a dragonfly

Susan Sanchez-Barnett

stepping stones—
the dragonfly always
one stone ahead

Patricia Neubauer

lotus to lotus
a dragonfly's shadow
lighter than air

Emily Romano

the pause
in a dragonfly's glide—
noon shadows

Kala Ramesh

indian paintbrush
colors the pond's edge
orange dragonflies

Renée Owen

restless morning
the dragonflies bob
along the path

Bob Lucky

morning coolness—
on the autumn grass
a dragonfly's wing

Origa

joined together
the second dragonfly rises
with the first

Jim Kacian

Photograph by Mike Rehling

neon blue
of a damselfly
fig leaf

Deborah P Kolodji

morning drizzle
blue butterflies settle
on the sundial

Elizabeth Howard

false dawn—
the one day
of the mayflies

Jim Kacian

last slices of moonshine—
silverside fish
in the mirror pool

Anatoly Kudryavitsky

spring thunder—
promising to meet
by the Monet

Peggy Willis Lyles

dried iris
by the zigzag bridge
a splash of koi

Deborah P Kolodji

the way
koi pleat the water
my lips open

Margaret Chula

as it rises
whiter and whiter
morning koi

Bruce Ross

zen garden
a bit of the sun
in the koi pond

Marie Summers

Zen garden—
goldfish and maple leaves
the same deep red

André Surridge

Photograph by Mike Rehling

carp suck
at the feeding hand . . . spring
in the temple pool

Carolyn Thomas

circling koi—
the lily pond nearly full
of water lettuce

Sharon Hammer Baker

marriage proposal
koi change
direction

Tony A. Thompson

lily pond
a carp scatters
pollen

Bozena Zernec

zen garden . . .
koi circle
the fallen leaves

Marie Summers

late afternoon
  carp whiskers
  reflect the sun

  Margaret Chula

lily pads—
tadpoles dart
through a shadow

  Emily Romano

warm summer night
he serenades goldfish
with his bamboo flute

  William Scott Galasso

frightened carp
the river silt
blossoms

Jim Kacian

two proud umbrellas
meeting on the footbridge
pass without pausing

Patricia Neubauer

a koi
noses the lily pad—
July afternoon

Deborah P Kolodji

leaf-strewn pond:
the cold shadow
of a fish

Carolyn Thomas

slow to be seated
—a fountain koi
spits up a pebble

Elliot Nicely

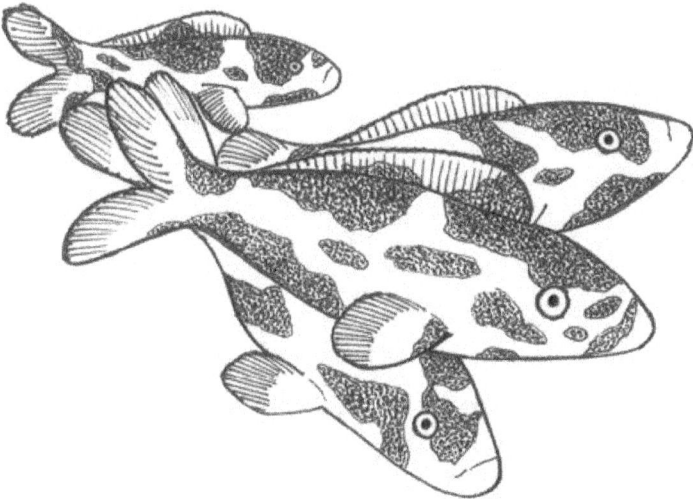

Artwork by Sandy Ellis

shady pool
a koi returns
my stare

Francis Masat

not all the bubbles
from a fish
pop

André Surridge

goldfish pond —
a flurry of orange
below the heron's shadow

Janelle Barrera

sunlight
on their backs . . .
circling koi

Emily Romano

baby koi
near the lily pad
summer shadows

Deborah P Kolodji

ice flecks
on azalea buds
the koi go deep

Peggy Willis Lyles

evening moon—
at this end of the pond
a small goldfish

Carolyn Thomas

sunlit pond—
the echo
of each tadpole

Stanford M. Forrester

watching the fish pond
fill up with shadows
a distant train

Margaret Chula

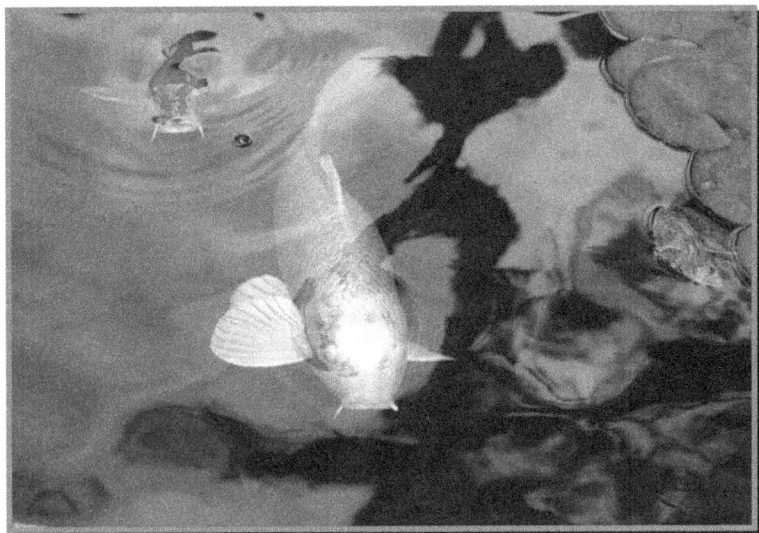

Photography by Mike Rehling

ancient carp
at the shallow's edge
a group of boys are silent

Glenn G. Coats

Hiroshima Day
in the friendship garden
flashes of koi

Deborah P Kolodji

water striders
skimming the koi pond
. . . one disappears

William Scott Galasso

humid night—
water bugs scurry
across the moon

Francis Masat

last iris—
circles of water striders
in the sun

Sharon Hammer Baker

temple path –
the small bridge vanishes
into a duckweed

Origa

water strider—
come this winter
I'll be you

George Dorsty

boys play-fight with cattails
all day she weeps

Tony A. Thompson

no croaks
from the cattails—
another year of drought

Renée Owen

summer breeze
cattails whisper where
water meets land

William Scott Galasso

pollen of a cattail
this brightness
just before sunset

Margaret Chula

cattails sway—
a distance runner passes
the silence between us

Tony A. Thompson

cattail slough
a slight seepage
in the heron's weave

Elizabeth Howard

a marshland shoal
encircled by reeds—
hoof tracks

Dusko Matas

letting go . . .
reeds crack
in this heat

Tony A. Thompson

Artwork by John Hawkhead

storks return . . .
first plum petals floating
in the marsh water

D. V. Rozic

evening shower
trees dripping
mosquitoes

Francis Masat

pond among the pines
a veil of floating pollen
arranged by the wind

Patricia Neubauer

Photo Haiga by Laryalee Fraser

a bent willow
in the water below it
one like it

Dubravko Korbus

silent marshland
a bird's feather hangs
on the reed

Zeljhka Vucinic-Jambresic

endless rain
the marsh swallows
its stumps

Dubravko Korbus

midwinter
the pond
in moonglow

Marie Summers

heat ripples—
pond willows lean
into their reflections

Marie Summers

white mist
covers the marsh—
summer's end

Milena Mrsic

endless rain
the willow is inhaled
by the water slowly

Dubravko Korbus

no grandchildren among the lily pads six white lotuses

Jan Turner

small boat fresh green on the pond

Jeffrey Stillman

purple twilight spilling frogs

Peggy Willis Lyles

pulling the cattail closer spider web

Tony A. Thompson

within the journey new awareness petal by petal

Haiga by Jan Turner

finding her note koi part the reeds

Tony A. Thompson

frog songs their splashing louder than the rain

Sharon Hammer Baker

through a maze of lilies brushstrokes of the trout

Peggy Willis Lyles

mist above the pond mosquitoes

Emily Romano

Tanka

pressing
my hands together
at the heart center —
somewhere in a pond
a lotus opens

Carolyn Thomas

The pond empty
of lotus blossoms;
like you and I,
the willows
don't quite touch.

alexis rotella

dew drops
on a lotus petal
bring memories —
tears
in her lovely eyes

Radhey Shiam

the lotus' beauty
is not for me—
deep down
I crave the root
tempura style

Bob Lucky

water lilies
reflecting the sky
we sit quietly
waiting for moonrise
over the dark pond

giselle maya

twilight
on water lilies
a nightingale
pleats his song
in shadow-play

Kala Ramesh

white splashes
of lilies in the pond
in growing darkness
frog choir gaining new voices
with every refrain

Origa

Pink petals
on the way
to the pond;
how easy it is
to just float.

alexis rotella

pond lilies
rising pearly white
from deep mud
i walk the shore wondering
am i able to do that . . .

giselle maya

the great blue heron
perches on a branch
two sizes too small—
a collective gasp
as it leaves us

Deborah P Kolodji

in the mist
the blue heron
slowly spreads its wings
and leaves behind the pond
as if it never was

Carolyn Thomas

feeling such peace
in this place, and yet
the bluegill
and the frog
fear the heron's shadow

James Rohrer

Photograph by Mike Rehling

lotus season
is coming to an end—
around the lake
seed pod vendors
drive a hard bargain

Bob Lucky

the flat pond—
are we not all frogs that sit
around its bank
waiting to experience
life's deeper dimension?

an'ya

last spring's golden koi
suspended beneath thick ice—
through days of hampered movement
sometimes the vague glimmer
of that imprisoned self

Linda Jeannette Ward

children
near the garden pond
feeding koi
this cloudy afternoon . . .
flashes of red and gold

Deborah P Kolodji

Photograph by Mike Rehling

a dragonfly
skims the surface
the quiet flutter
        lying next to you
        even after all these years

Elinor Pihl Huggett

blue damselfly
over the water lilies
this summer day
currents swirl below
with my daydreams

Deborah P Kolodji

dragonfly
by last evening light
drinks from pond water—
in the stillness, the moon
hangs silent

Carolyn Thomas

Back then, grandpa
plucked cattails from a lily pond
and lit their ends . . .
we were wild Indians
bringing home the fire

George Dorsty

somewhere
there's that lost sister who's
also grown old . . . ice
at the pond's edges
opens to patterns of lace

Linda Jeannette Ward

At the crowded party,
the way your body
slid past mine—
koi in a late
autumn pond.

alexis rotella

the full moon
trembling in a cold depth
of April water;
an owl's hollow hoot
somewhere across the pond

Origa

scarlet branches
of the maple mirrored
in the pond
suddenly set a-sway
by arriving white ducks

Amelia Fielden

The old tire swing
over a South Dakota pond
taking what's left
of the girl-child in me
deep into its secret world

an'ya

snow moon
twilit lavender blue
on the millpond
i float your ashes
among drifting swans

Linda Jeannette Ward

Photograph by Mike Rehling

Bamboo growing
through slats
of a wooden bridge,
faster than the bicycles
can trim it.

alexis rotella

a broken stem
of agapanthus
bobs in the wind —
my sigh as I think of you
when no one is listening

Deborah P Kolodji

Inner courtyard—
heavenly bamboo
in turquoise pots;
the dark green tea
I brew for two.

alexis rotella

Two dragonflies
weave through the cattails,
Spring mating . . .
we text message our rituals
between your flights to Paris.

Bette Wappner (b'oki)

after the kingfisher
stillness returns to the pond
like love cut into pieces
the wound closes
minus a few precious drops

Linda Jeannette Ward

Photograph by Mike Rehling

across the lake
lotuses are in bloom—
buried in mud
tourists at the spa
seek the key to beauty

Bob Lucky

Index

Acknowledgements

an'ya: "breast high" *Jack Stamm Contest*; "The old tire swing" *SGL*

Baker, W.: "a dragonfly" *Frogpond XVIII:2*

Berry: "lily pad" and "lily pond" *The webWorks Gallery (webWorks haiku #22)*
Bowman: "dragonfly . . ." *White Lotus, Spring/Summer 2008, Issue 6*

Chula: "late afternoon," "watching the fish pond," old woman" and "decayed leaves" *Grinding my ink*; "pollen of a cattail," "reflecting" and "the way" *The Smell of Rust*

Dolphy: "lotus lilies" *Presence #24*

Forrester: "for a moment" and "summer rain . . ." *Daily Yomiuri, October 2005 (Japan)*; "sunlit pond—" *Mayfly, Vol. 22, Issue 44*

Fraser: "drift of daylight" *Haigaonline, issue 7-2, autumn/winter 2006*

Hawkhead: "at the pond's centre" *Presence 29*; "slow bend in the stream—" *Presence 33*

Howard: "willows greening" *Modern Haiku XXXII:2*; "cattail slough" *The Heron's Nest V:11*

Kolodji: "orange dragonfly" *tinywords 8/7/2007*; "Hiroshima Day" *tinywords 8/6/2007*; "baby koi" *Mainichi Daily News, Sept. 2006*; "a koi" *bottle rockets, Vol. 9, No. 2*; "floating purple—" *2007 Yuki Teikei Society Membership Anthology*; "children" *Simply Haiku, Vol. 4, No. 2*; "blue damselfly" and "a broken stem" *Modern English Tanka, Vol. 1, No. 1*

Kacian: "frightened carp" *ant5 3*; "twilight" *Honolulu Advertiser*; "the whole pond" *Hobo 14*; "midsummer heat" *odzaci 2003*; "false dawn—" *Cicada 24*

Kudryavitsky: "summer night—" *2005 Samhain International Haiku Competition*; "last slices of moonshine—" *Morning at Mount Ring*

Lyles: "a lily bud" *10th Annual Suruga Baika Literary Festival Award, 2008*; "through a maze," "dragonfly . . ." and "ice flecks" *To Hear the Rain, Brooks Books 2008*; "morning mist—" *Mayfly #38*; "spring thunder—" *bottle rockets #9*; "purple twilight" *Modern Haiku XVII:3*

Masat: "a heron's eye" *Simply Haiku, Autumn 2006*; "shady pool" and "humid night—" *clouds peak, August 2006*; "evening shower" *Simply Haiku, January 2004*; "evening star—" *Wisteria, April 2008*

Millcock & Sananda: "your song" (haiga) *pausing for a moment*

Moldovan: "diving messenger" *Mainichi Daily News, July 2006*; "before the storm" *clouds peak, 2006*

Neubauer: "pond among the pines" *Mainichi Daily News, June 2004*; "two proud umbrellas" *Modern Haiku XVIII:3*; "toy warship" *Haiku International #18*; "stepping stones" *Mainichi Daily News, 2003*; "far from the pond" *Frogpond XVI:2*

Origa: "morning coolness—" *Modern Haiku Vol. 38.2*; "Cranes" (haiga) and "Frog and dragonfly" (haiga) *Lishanu, 2005*; "Heron" (haiga) *Simply Haiku, Vol. 4, No. 4*; "Lazy Afternoon" (haiga) *WHA Haiga Contest, 2006*

Romano: "lotus to lotus" *taken from "Lotus Enlightenment," a haibun, White Lotus, Fall/Winter 2005, Issue 1*

Rotella: "Inner courtyard—" *Elvis in Black Leather*; "At the crowded party" and "Bamboo growing" *Lip Prints*; "The pond empty" *Lace Curtain*; "In fading light" *Eavesdropping*

Sanchez-Barnett: "by a lily pad" *White Lotus, Issue 6*

Summers: "news of your illness . . ." *Wisteria, Issue 8*; "thick fog" *Lynx, June 2005*; "shiny penny . . ." Nisqually Delta Review, Vol. 3, Issue 3; "zen garden" *Haiku Harvest, Vol. 6, No. 1*; "midwinter" *Haiku Scotland, June 2006*; "zen garden . . ." and "lighter than water" *clouds peak, July 2006*

Surridge: "pond edge—" *Valley Micropress, 2006*; "Zen garden—" *World Kigo web site*

Thomas: "leaf-strewn pond: " *Persimmon, Vol. 2, No. 2* and *puddle on the ink stone*; "in the mist" *Tundra #2, The Tanka Anthology 2003, puddle on the ink stone* and *Countless Leaves*; "carp suck" *Honolulu Advertiser, Spring 1983*; "night" *The Poetry Conspiracy, Vol.6.3*; "two blue dragonflies" *Timepieces, 1997*; "evening moon—" *Geppo Vol. XXII:3*; "dragonfly" *American Tanka, Issue 4* and *puddle on the ink stone*; "pressing" *puddle on the ink stone*

Turner: "lotus rising—" *White Lotus, Fall/Winter 2005, Issue 1*

Ward: "sultry afternoon—" *Frogpond XXII:3*; "snow moon" *Northeast, 2003*; "somewhere" *Eucalypt #3*; "last spring's golden koi" *Blithe Spirit, Vol. 13* and *Scent of Jasmine and Brine, 2007*; "after the kingfisher" *Yellow Moon #19*

Zernec: "lily pond" and "moonlight" *A Carp in the Clouds*; morning blossom" and "fragile water-lilies" *Look!*